COUNTRY EXPLORERS

SOUTH KOREA

Jennifer A. Miller

Lerner Publications Company • Minneapolis

W9-CEK-881

Lerner Publications Company
A division of Lerner Publishing Group, Inc.
241 First Avenue North
Minneapolis, MN 55401 U.S.A.

Website address: www.lernerbooks.com

Library of Congress Cataloging-in-Publication Data

Miller, Jennifer A.
    South Korea / by Jennifer A. Miller.
        p. cm. — (Country explorers)
    Includes index.
    ISBN 978–1–58013–605–1 (lib. bdg. : alk. paper)
    1. Korea (South)—Juvenile literature. I. Title.
DS902.12.M55 2010
951.95—dc22   2009020566

Manufactured in the United States of America
1 – VI – 12/15/09

jj 915.195

Table of Contents

Welcome!

We're taking a trip to South Korea. This country is part of the continent of Asia. South Korea and its neighbor North Korea make up the Korea Peninsula. (A peninsula has water on three sides.) North of the peninsula are China and Russia. Japan lies across the sea to the south and east.

South Korea

South Korea has many ancient temples.

country's capital
mountains
plains

NORTH KOREA

DEMILITARIZED ZONE

N

Seoul

HAN RIVER

TAEBAEK MOUNTAINS

MILES
0   50   100
0   50   100   150
KILOMETERS

YELLOW SEA

SOUTH
KOREA

SOUTHWESTERN PLAIN

GEUM RIVER

Boryeong

RUSSIA

CHINA

NORTH KOREA

SEA OF JAPAN

ULLEUNGDO

SOUTH KOREA

JAPAN

JEJU ISLAND

SOBAEK MOUNTAINS

BOMUN LAKE

NAKDONG RIVER

SOUTHERN PLAIN

KOREA STRAIT

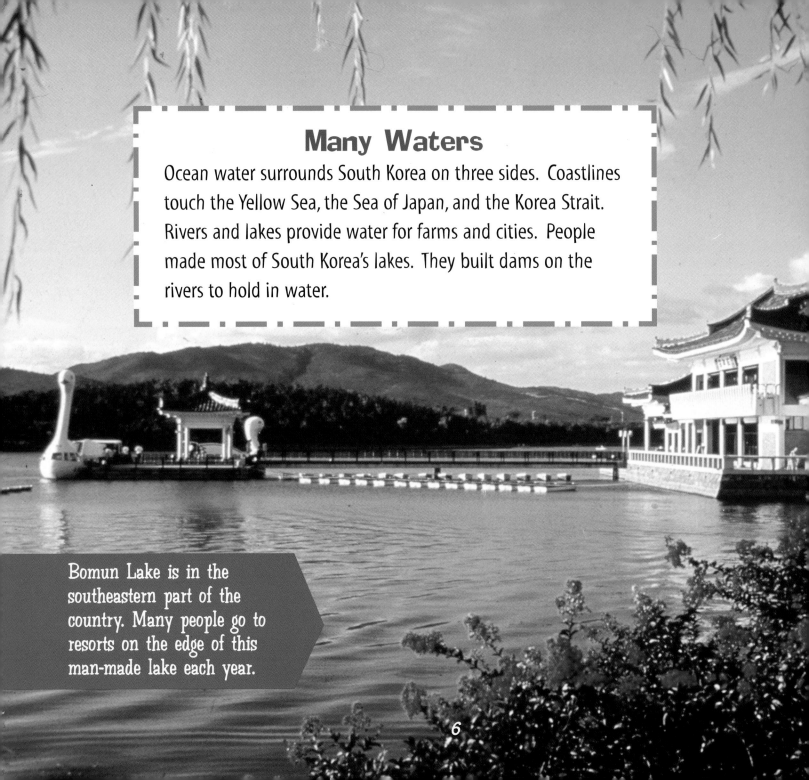

Many Waters

Ocean water surrounds South Korea on three sides. Coastlines touch the Yellow Sea, the Sea of Japan, and the Korea Strait. Rivers and lakes provide water for farms and cities. People made most of South Korea's lakes. They built dams on the rivers to hold in water.

Bomun Lake is in the southeastern part of the country. Many people go to resorts on the edge of this man-made lake each year.

Mud Baths

Many people visit mudflats on the western coast of South Korea. People cover their bodies with the thick mud found there. They do this to relax and make their skin healthier. Then they rinse off in the Yellow Sea.

A mud festival is held each July in Boryeong. Many Koreans and tourists travel to Boryeong to take part in mud-filled activities.

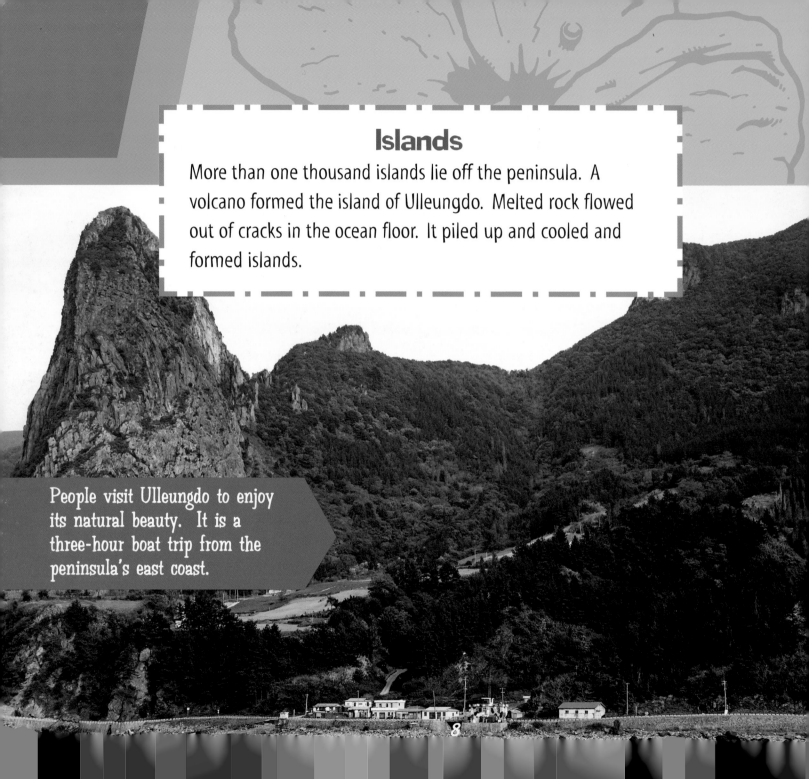

Islands

More than one thousand islands lie off the peninsula. A volcano formed the island of Ulleungdo. Melted rock flowed out of cracks in the ocean floor. It piled up and cooled and formed islands.

People visit Ulleungdo to enjoy its natural beauty. It is a three-hour boat trip from the peninsula's east coast.

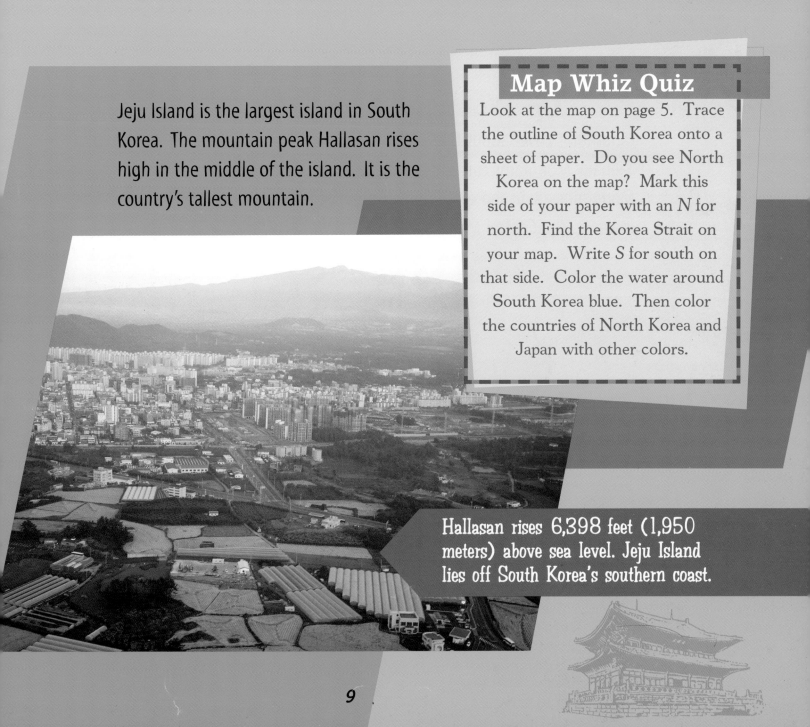

Jeju Island is the largest island in South Korea. The mountain peak Hallasan rises high in the middle of the island. It is the country's tallest mountain.

Map Whiz Quiz

Look at the map on page 5. Trace the outline of South Korea onto a sheet of paper. Do you see North Korea on the map? Mark this side of your paper with an N for north. Find the Korea Strait on your map. Write S for south on that side. Color the water around South Korea blue. Then color the countries of North Korea and Japan with other colors.

Hallasan rises 6,398 feet (1,950 meters) above sea level. Jeju Island lies off South Korea's southern coast.

Up High and Down Low

Mountains cover about three-fourths of South Korea. The Taebaek Mountains run along the east coast. The Sobaek Mountains are in the center of the country. These two ranges make up the Central Mountains.

The Sobaek Mountains include the tallest peak on South Korea's mainland.

South Korea also has plains and lowlands. The Southwestern Plain and Southern Plain include rich farmland.

These people are working in a rice field in the Southwestern Plain.

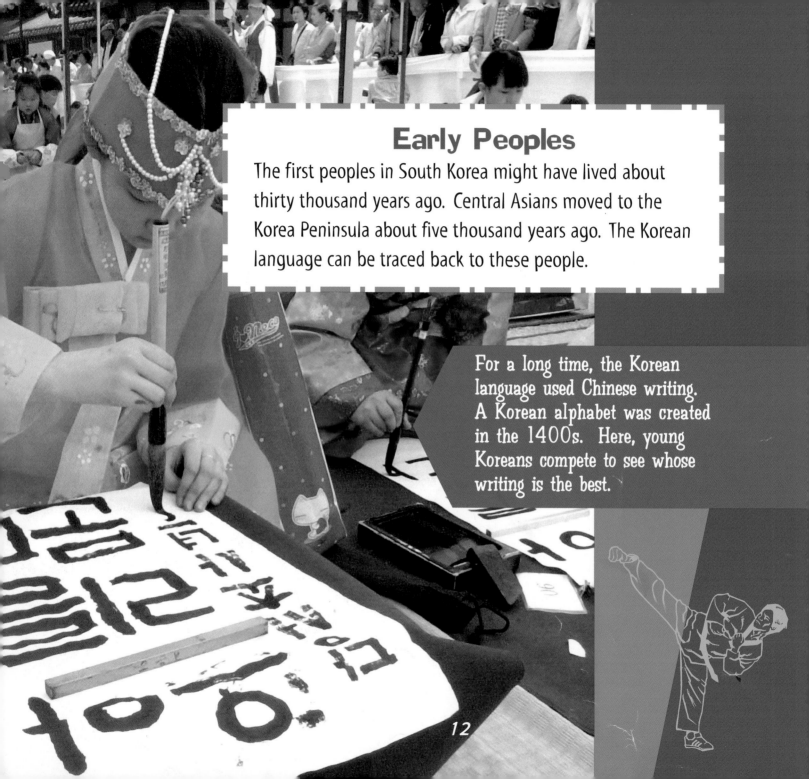

Early Peoples

The first peoples in South Korea might have lived about thirty thousand years ago. Central Asians moved to the Korea Peninsula about five thousand years ago. The Korean language can be traced back to these people.

For a long time, the Korean language used Chinese writing. A Korean alphabet was created in the 1400s. Here, young Koreans compete to see whose writing is the best.

Ancient tools and pottery hold clues about the lives of the first South Koreans. These early people hunted, fished, and gathered food. Later, they farmed the land.

Legend: The Founding Father of Korea

According to legend, the ancient leader Dangun started the Joseon dynasty (ruling family) more than 4,000 years ago. This time is thought of as the beginning of Korea. The story says Dangun lived for another one thousand years. He then became a mountain god. Koreans celebrate Dangun Day on October 3 as the day he founded Korea.

Historians dig up ancient tombs in South Korea. Tools and objects they find help them learn about the early Koreans.

Capital City

Seoul is the capital of South Korea. It lies on the Han River. About ten million people live in this crowded city.

Seoul has a lot to see and do. Visitors get a good view of the city from N Seoul Tower. If you like art and history, check out the National Museum of Korea or Seoul's palaces and temples. And shoppers can find almost anything in the Namdaemun Market or the modern COEX Mall.

Many people crowd into the Namdaemun Market in downtown Seoul every day.

14

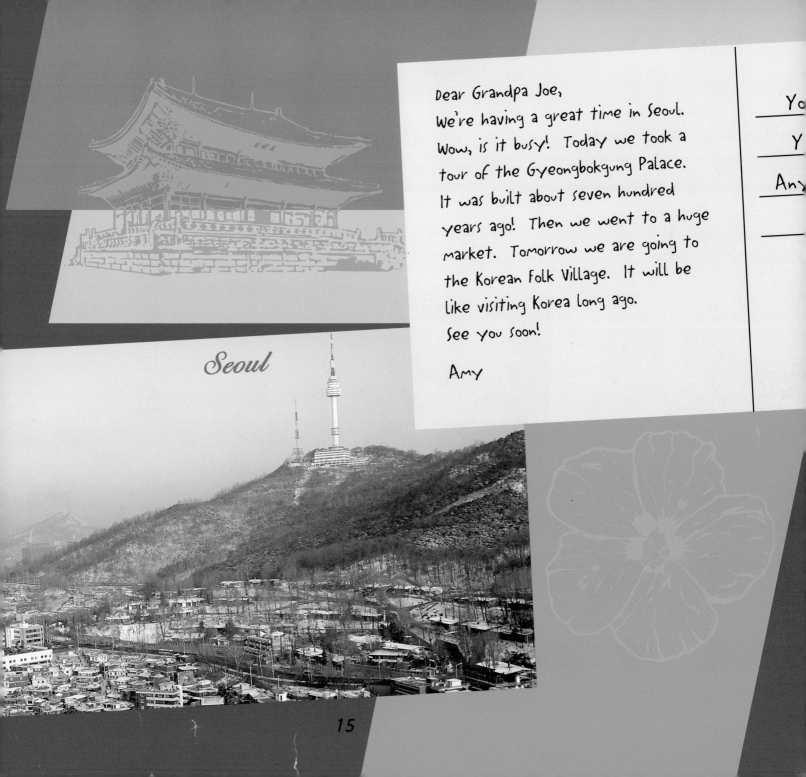

Seoul

Dear Grandpa Joe,
We're having a great time in Seoul.
Wow, is it busy! Today we took a
tour of the Gyeongbokgung Palace.
It was built about seven hundred
years ago! Then we went to a huge
market. Tomorrow we are going to
the Korean Folk Village. It will be
like visiting Korea long ago.
See you soon!

Amy

Yo
Y
Any

15

Families

Family is very important in South Korea. In the past, grandparents, parents, and children lived in one house. Usually just the parents and children live together in modern times.

Korean families eat together at tables on the floor.

Did You Know?

Korean names have three parts. First is the family name. The second part is sometimes shared by all brothers or all sisters. The third part is what we call our first name. Sometimes this is connected to the second part. So the name Jennifer Annette Miller might look like "Miller Annette-jennifer" in Korean. What would your name look like?

Many couples have only one or two children. Few mothers have jobs outside the home. They choose to stay home with their children. Fathers work long hours so their families have enough money.

17

Respect

Respect is important to South Koreans. Children respect and obey their parents. Wives respect their husbands. Younger people respect older people.

South Korean children respect and listen to their teachers.

18

These ideas came from a set of beliefs called Confucianism. Confucianism teaches that everyone has a proper place in society. The beliefs also include rules for good behavior.

Confucianism started with the teachings of Confucius. He was a man who lived about 2,500 years ago in China.

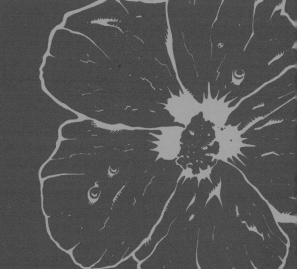

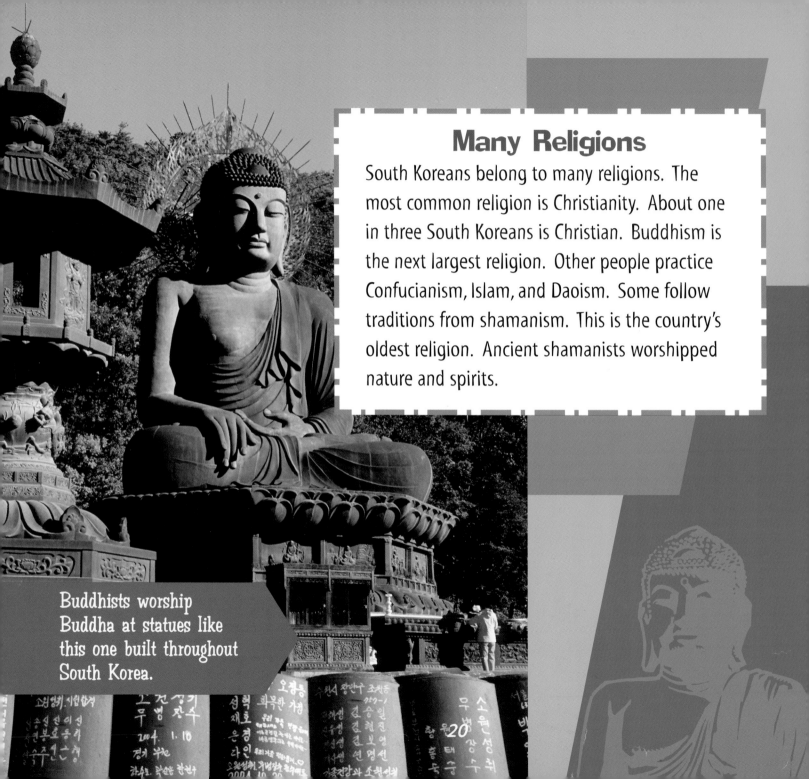

Many Religions

South Koreans belong to many religions. The most common religion is Christianity. About one in three South Koreans is Christian. Buddhism is the next largest religion. Other people practice Confucianism, Islam, and Daoism. Some follow traditions from shamanism. This is the country's oldest religion. Ancient shamanists worshipped nature and spirits.

Buddhists worship Buddha at statues like this one built throughout South Korea.

Christians worship in Myeongdong Cathedral in Seoul.

Holidays and Festivals

South Koreans enjoy holidays and traditional festivals. The Lunar New Year is an important holiday. It is called Seollal. People honor their ancestors and their oldest family members during this celebration. Chuseok is a fall holiday. South Koreans give thanks for a good harvest on this day.

Children fly kites as part of the Lunar New Year celebration.

22

Koreans celebrate Chuseok by eating a special meal.

Holidays

January 1	New Year's Day
January/February	Lunar New Year
March 1	Independence Movement Day
April/May	Buddha's Birthday
May 5	Children's Day
June 6	Memorial Day
July 17	Constitution Day
August 15	Liberation Day
September/October	Chuseok
October 3	National Foundation Day (Dangun Day)
December 25	Christmas Day

This man is eating *bulgogi*, a Korean barbecue.

Let's Eat!

Every South Korean meal includes white rice and a pickled vegetable dish called kimchi. Vegetables and chicken, fish, or beef may be part of the meal too. But rice is the main course. Koreans eat their meals at a low table. Everyone sits on the floor. They use spoons to eat soup and rice. They eat other food with chopsticks. Have you ever tried eating with chopsticks?

Kimchi

Kimchi is the national dish of South Korea. Pickled vegetables and red pepper are the basic ingredients. But there are more than one hundred different kinds of kimchi. People serve at least two kinds with every meal.

This buffet has many kinds of kimchi.

Time for School

Education is very important to South Koreans. Students work hard at school and on homework. They study math, science, social studies, music and art, and Korean. They also learn other languages such as English and Chinese.

Students work at their desks in a classroom in Seoul.

All students finish junior high. Then most go to high school. In the last year of high school, students take an all-day test. Their scores on that exam decide which college they can attend.

These students are taking their college entrance exam. Many high school students spend every evening studying for this test.

Sports

Tae kwon do is the country's most popular sport. It was created in Korea more than two thousand years ago. It became an Olympic sport in 2000.

Tae kwon do is South Korea's national sport.

28

Archery and wrestling are other traditional Korean sports. Korean wrestling is called *ssireum*. Soccer is also popular.

Ssireum is the oldest sport in South Korea.

Crafts

Korean crafts are known for their beautiful designs. Celadon is a famous kind of pottery from Korea. *Bojagi* are colorful square cloths. They are made in different sizes to wrap, store, or carry things. Crafts made from wood or paper are popular too. Paper lanterns decorate houses, temples, and streets.

These vases are examples of South Korean celadon pottery.

Hanbok

South Koreans wear modern clothes for daily life. But for special occasions, they wear traditional clothing called *hanbok*. Both men and women wear these colorful, loose clothes. Some Korean fashion designers are making new versions of hanbok.

Music

Koreans enjoy traditional and modern music. In *pansori* music, a singer performs long storytelling songs while a drummer plays a *buk* (a barrel drum). Other traditional instruments include a *gayageum* (a long, flat box with twelve strings) and a *jing* (a large gong).

A man beats a buk during a traditional farmers dance.

Men at a folk festival play traditional Korean instruments.

South Koreans also like classical music, opera, pop, hip-hop, and rhythm and blues. The artist known as Rain *(right)* is one of the country's biggest pop stars.

At Home

Many older homes in South Korea were made of clay and wood. Newer houses are built with concrete. In cities, most people live in apartment buildings because space is limited.

Four out of five South Koreans live in a city.

Most South Koreans sleep on mats on the floor. This is the traditional way. But some people have beds.

Did You Know?
Most homes have an ancient heating system under their floors. This is why Koreans eat and sleep on the floor, where it is warm. To keep floors clean, they always take off their shoes before coming inside.

A Love of Nature

South Koreans love their land and the environment. They build their homes or offices to face the water or to catch breezes. They like to relax in gardens. Gardens are near homes, office buildings, and cities. National parks also protect areas of natural land.

The rose of Sharon is South Korea's national flower. It is a type of hibiscus.

Visitors hike through the Seoraksan National Park in northeastern South Korea.

In the Wild

Many kinds of wildlife are at home in South Korea. Wild boars and deer are common. Asiatic black bears, tigers, leopards, and wolves used to roam the mountains and forests. But few are left. In 2003, scientists discovered a new animal in South Korea's forests. It is a type of salamander.

The Asiatic black bear is an endangered species in South Korea.

The crane is a symbol of good luck for South Koreans. Red-crowned cranes are large. They stand about 5 feet (1.5 m) high.

More than four hundred birds spend time in South Korea. Off the coast, sharks, squid, and octopuses are at home in the seas. Carps, eels, smelt, and trout swim in the lakes.

North vs. South

The Korea Peninsula was split into South Korea and North Korea after World War II (1939–1945). In 1950, North Korea invaded South Korea. This started the Korean War. The war ended in 1953. But the two countries are still divided.

Lee Myung-bak became the president of South Korea in 2008.

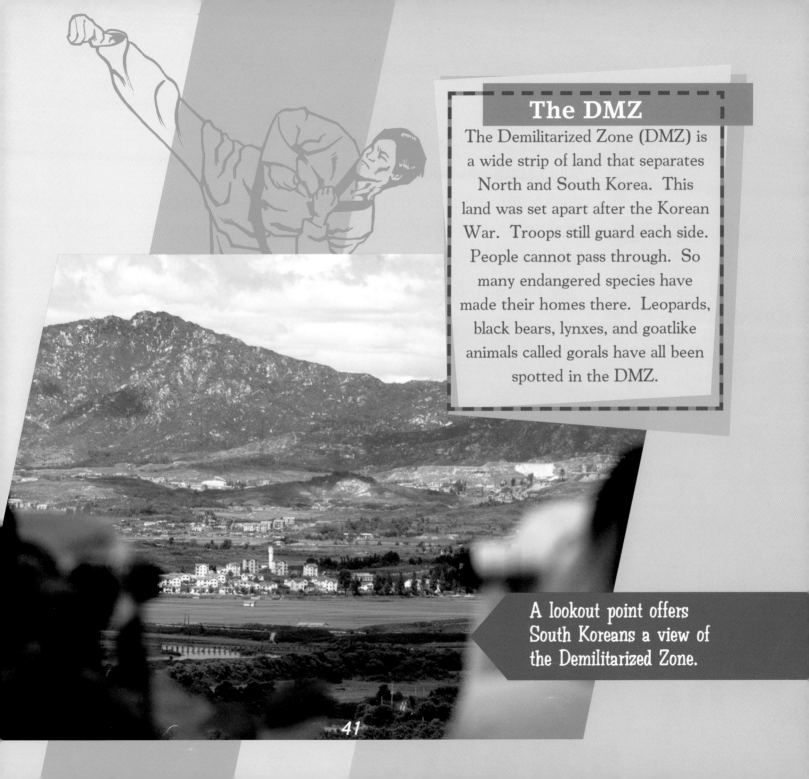

The DMZ

The Demilitarized Zone (DMZ) is a wide strip of land that separates North and South Korea. This land was set apart after the Korean War. Troops still guard each side. People cannot pass through. So many endangered species have made their homes there. Leopards, black bears, lynxes, and goatlike animals called gorals have all been spotted in the DMZ.

A lookout point offers South Koreans a view of the Demilitarized Zone.

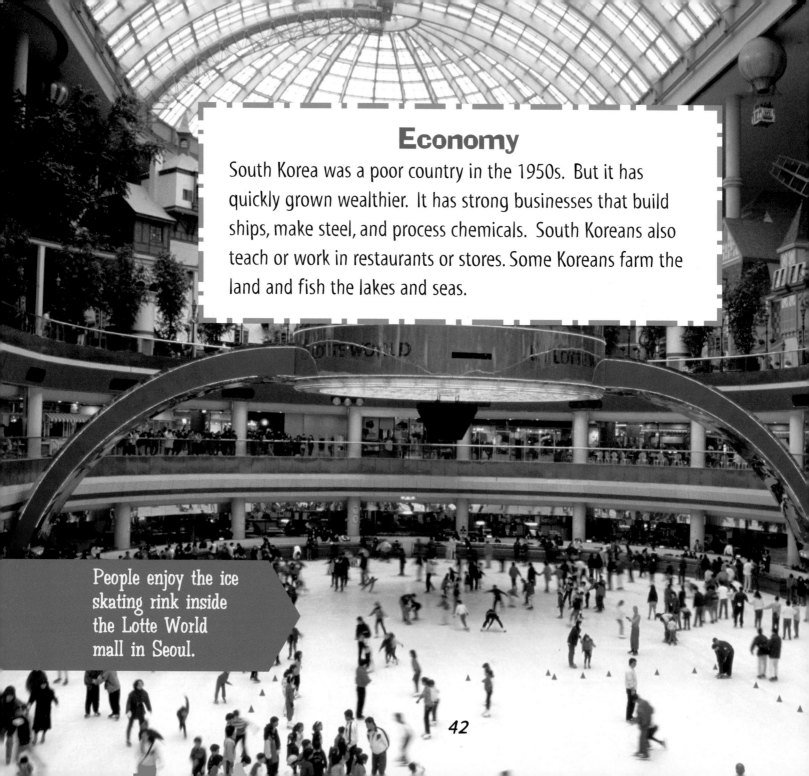

Economy

South Korea was a poor country in the 1950s. But it has quickly grown wealthier. It has strong businesses that build ships, make steel, and process chemicals. South Koreans also teach or work in restaurants or stores. Some Koreans farm the land and fish the lakes and seas.

People enjoy the ice skating rink inside the Lotte World mall in Seoul.

42

Have you heard of Samsung or LG electronics? Or Hyundai cars? These are Korean products. Many of these goods are sent to other countries.

This Hyundai Avante LPI is a hybrid car made in South Korea. It runs partly on electricity and partly on gas. So it uses less gas than most cars.

THE FLAG OF SOUTH KOREA

South Korea's flag is called the Taegeukgi. It became the official flag of South Korea in 1950. The red and blue circle stands for the two opposite forces in the universe. The set of lines in the upper left means heaven. The lines in the bottom right stand for earth. The lines in the lower left mean fire, while the lines in the upper right stand for water. The white background stands for the purity of the Korean people in their love of peace.

FAST FACTS

Full Country Name: Republic of Korea

Area: 38,022 square miles (98,477 square kilometers), or about the same size as Indiana

MAIN LANDFORMS: the Central Mountain region, including the mountain ranges of Taebaek and Sobaek; the Southwestern Plain; the Southern Plain

MAJOR RIVERS: Nakdong, Han, Geum

ANIMALS AND THEIR HABITATS: wild pony, roe deer (Jeju Island); salamander, wild boar, deer, red fox (woods); Manchurian crane, seagull, sea hawk, egret (coast); abalone, shark, squid, octopus (ocean); carp, eel, trout (lakes)

CAPITAL CITY: Seoul

OFFICIAL LANGUAGE: Korean

POPULATION: about 49,045,000

GLOSSARY

ancestors: relatives who lived long ago

capital: a city where the government is located

continent: any one of seven large areas of land. The continents are Africa, Antarctica, Asia, Australia, Europe, North America, and South America.

lowland: an area that is lower than the surrounding land

map: a drawing or chart of all or part of Earth or the sky

mountain range: a group of mountains

peninsula: an area of land with water on three sides

plain: a large area of flat land

religion: a system of belief and worship

strait: a narrow passage of water connecting two large bodies of water

volcano: an opening in Earth's surface through which hot, melted rock shoots up. Volcano can also refer to the hill or mountain that builds up around the opening.

TO LEARN MORE

BOOKS

Cheung, Hyechong. *K Is for Korea.* London: Frances Lincoln Children's Books, 2008. This book uses the alphabet to introduce readers to Korea's culture.

Haskins, Jim. *Count Your Way through Korea.* Minneapolis: Millbrook Press, 1989. In this colorful picture book, you'll learn more about Korea, from its buildings and food to its language.

Jackson, Tom. *South Korea.* Washington, DC: National Geographic, 2007. Find out how South Korea became a wealthy nation, who Kim Dae-jung was, and how a typhoon affected the country.

Walters, Tara. *South Korea.* New York: Children's Press, 2008. South Korea's culture, traditions, and much more are explored in this book.

WEBSITES

Confucius—History for Kids! http://www.historyforkids.org/learn/ china/philosophy/confucius2.htm The ideas of Confucius, who lived long ago, are still an important part of Korean culture. Visit this site to read about his life and teachings.

National Geographic Kids http://kids.nationalgeographic.com/ Places/Find/South-korea Loaded with photos and videos, this site also provides facts and a map.

Time for Kids around the World http://www.timeforkids.com/TFK/kids/ hh/goplaces/main/0,28375,927166,00 .html This site features a map, fun facts, and a historical timeline of South Korea.

INDEX